Peter Spurway's
Practical, Powerful *and* Effective Guide *to* Media Relations

Peter Spurway's PRACTICAL, POWERFUL *and* EFFECTIVE GUIDE *to* MEDIA RELATIONS

Get Past the Fear and Use the Control You
Don't Realize You Have to Deliver Your Message Effectively,
Every Chance You Get

PETER SPURWAY

Copyright © 2017 by Peter Spurway.

Library of Congress Control Number:		2017902966
ISBN:	Hardcover	978-1-5245-8672-0
	Softcover	978-1-5245-8673-7
	eBook	978-1-5245-8674-4

All rights reserved. No part of this book may be reproduced or transmitted in any form or by any means, electronic or mechanical, including photocopying, recording, or by any information storage and retrieval system, without permission in writing from the copyright owner.

Any people depicted in stock imagery provided by Thinkstock are models, and such images are being used for illustrative purposes only.
Certain stock imagery © Thinkstock.

Print information available on the last page.

Rev. date: 03/14/2017

To order additional copies of this book, contact:
Xlibris
1-888-795-4274
www.Xlibris.com
Orders@Xlibris.com
756874

Contents

A

Accessibility 1
Accuracy 2
Acronyms (Use of) 3
Adversary 3
Advisors 4
Agenda 4
Aiding and Abetting 5
Anger 5
Anticipation 6
Attribution (Not for) 7
Availability 8

B

Background (See also Patience) ... 9
Basics 9
Brevity 10
Bridging 10

C

Changing Face of the Media 13
Clarity 13
Clips 14
Comment? 14
Comments (Online) 15
Commitments 15
Communication (Test of Effective) 16
Complaints 16

Conflict 17
Control 18
Corrections/Clarifications 19
Creating your own Content 19
Credibility 20
Crisis and Opportunity 20

D

Deadlines 23
Deafness 23
Delivery 24
Double-ender 25

E

Educating Reporters 27
Editorials 27
Ego 27
Energy and Emotion 28
Engaging the Media 28
Equal Treatment 29
Errors (Omission, Commission) ... 30
Examples 30
Exhaustion 31
Exit Strategy 31
Experience 32

F

Facts 35
Fairness 35

"Found" Information 36
Friends 36
Full Disclosure 37

G

Guarantees 39
Goal 39
Grammar 39

H

Heart 41
Honesty 41

I

Interview 45
Introduction (Your) 45
Issue versus Crisis 46

J

Jargon (Use of) 47

K

Key Messages 49
Know the Audience 49
Know Your Stuff 50

L

Language (Vocabulary) 53
Legal Advice 54
Legs 55
Lies 55
Listen 56

Long Form Interview 56
Luck 57

M

Managing Expectations 59
Media 59
Media Conference 59
Media Relations 60
Monitoring 60
Multiple Interviews (Same day, Same topic) 60

N

Newsworthy 63
"No Comment" 63
Nuance 64
Numbers 64

O

Objectivity (and Unicorns) 67
"Off the Record" 67
On the Record 68

P

Paranoia (Healthy) 69
Patience 69
Person 69
Permanence 70
Personality 70
Pitch and Pace (and Tone) 70
Practice 71
Press 71

Preparation (General) 71
Preparation (Specific) 72
Print 73
Proactive versus Reactive 74

Q

Questions 75

R

Radio 77
Recording the interview 78
Refusing 78
Relationship 79
Role of the Media 79

S

Saying No, Thank You 81
Scrums 81
Simplicity 82
Social Media 82
Speculation 82
Speed 83
Staking Your Claim 83
Stereotypes 84

T

Take Five 85
Take Two 85
Ts (The Three) 86
Thank You 86
The Rule 87
The Rule for Communications Advisors 87

Tone 88
Traps and Tricks 88
Trust 89
Truth 90
Two Voices 90

U

Unusual 93

V

Vacuum Theory 95
Verbal Cue 95
Video (TV, Podcast, Skype, etc. versus Print) 96
Visualization 97

W

When You Get It Wrong 99
When You're Not Your Best 100
Who Speaks When? 100
Why Care? 100

X

X-Rated 103

Y

Yes or No 105

Z

Zen 107

Media Relations 101 109

Dedication

To good communications advisors who understand the value of a solid working relationship with the media and who respect reporters and the difficult job they do.

To good reporters who pursue the truth with fairness and accuracy and who understand that organizations don't exist to provide them with stories.

As Dan Rather so eloquently wrote:

"Be skeptical but not cynical, dogged but not disrespectful, confrontational but not oppositional. Your job is to try to get to as close to a version of the truth as is humanly possible. Pull no punches. Do not succumb to fear or favor. Present what you have found to your readers, listeners and viewers and let them draw their own conclusions."

Introduction

Way too many people are afraid of the media.

What do they want? What will they ask? Why can't they just leave us alone?

Be not afraid. The answers to these and many other questions are inside.

You *can* discern the media's motives. You *can* anticipate what they'll ask. And you *can* be well-prepared to answer their questions and advance your agenda.

And it's not half as hard as you might think.

The fact of the matter is that a solid, professional working relationship with the media is in your company/organization/

brand's (COB's) best interests – especially when things go wrong. And they will go wrong.

This solid, professional working relationship also comes in very handy when you want to talk about your latest/greatest product/service.

This practical, powerful, handy, simple and effective guide will show you how to use the control you don't realize you have to manage your relationship with the media to your benefit and theirs.

You will learn how to prepare and deliver your messages effectively, even in a hostile environment when the chips are down.

Why this Relationship Matters

Effective media relations is critical to building awareness about your company/organization/brand (COB). Supportive media stories can be valuable third party endorsements and can position your COB as a valuable contributor to the life and growth of your community, with so much more credibility than any advertising you may do.

Your goal is not simply to supply useful, newsworthy information to media outlets, but to build trust and good faith in your working relationship with them.

A good relationship with the media is based on trust and honesty. There will be the odd reporter who may violate these principles, but they can be managed.

Good reporters are always looking for help in understanding the situations about which they are reporting. If you can provide that help in a trustworthy, timely and straightforward way, you are in a position to develop a good working relationship with reporters and help them understand what your COB is all about.

Your goal is to *manage* your relationship with the media, because you cannot *control* it.

You are one half of a relationship, and you have complete control of your side of the equation. Use that control to your advantage. You have what they want - and they have access to audiences valuable to you.

How to Use this Book

This book is in aphabetical order.

You should be able to find any topic listed in the Contents within a few seconds.

Or you can open it anywhere.

On second thought, start by re-reading the Introduction and Why this Relationship Matters. That'll help establish the base on which the book is written - that your relationship with the media is a relationship worth the investment.

Important themes will be repeated throughout the book, appearing in several places.

A

Accessibility

If you or your COB (company/organization/brand) issue a media release, make sure there's a media contact person listed, and make darn sure they are available for the next 48 hours or so.

And if there are people in your COB who are quoted in the release, ensure *they* are available as well.

If your COB is large enough, especially if your operation never closes (airport, hospital, political office, etc.), one of your media relations folks needs to be on call 24/7.

Simply having a human being answering the phone, text or email and trying to be helpful goes a long way to improving your relationship with the media.

As to who, besides your media relations person, is made available to the media, the subject matter expert is your best bet. Marketing story? VP or Director of Marketing. Financing? CFO. New facility? Planning/infrastructure VP or Director. You get the idea.

Do not put your CEO out there every time you burp. Save them for when it really counts - either the story is big enough, or has escalated to a point at which the big gun needs to roll out and put a definitive stamp on the matter.

I believe I have earned some respect from reporters simply by answering the phone when things were tough for my COB, or on the weekend, or in the middle of the night. There were many times when I didn't want to, believe me. But it's part of the relationship-building. You've got to, if you want them to take you seriously. You get points for it, but you get real points when you can stand and deliver in the firestorm of a major media crisis.

Accuracy

The two qualities that you can reasonably expect from your encounters with the media are *accuracy* and *fairness*. Did they get the facts right? Were they fair in their presentation of the story? Was there an apparent bias?

There is no such thing as objectivity. Reporters, despite what they might tell you, or wish to believe, are not objective. They bring a set of biases to every story they cover. They are human, after all. They like some things and don't like others. They particularly don't like people who lie to them and treat them badly. Then again, *we* don't like people who lie to us and treat us badly. (PS – if you enjoy being lied to and being treated badly, there is help out there for you. Get it.)

Reporters may like you or your COB, which can be useful. Or they may not like you. That makes your job harder – still doable, but harder.

A fair bit of the media's attitude toward your COB is based on how you treat them. The correlation is simple and direct – treat them badly, they will go out of their way to make trouble for you; treat them well and they will at least listen to you explain yourself after you've done something stupid, or at least when you appear to have done something stupid.

It's always stunning to see COBs who seem hell-bent on making reporter's lives difficult. And then they wonder why the media is so hard on them.

You need them, they need you. This inter-dependency is a big opportunity for you.

It's a *relationship*. Do your part.

But please, never expect them to be completely objective. You'll be disappointed every time.

Acronyms (Use of)

As a general rule, don't. They simply confuse your audience.

Speak in plain language.

Remember – if your audience doesn't understand what you're saying and therefore can't use the information you're providing, you're not communicating effectively. Keep it simple.

Adversary

There will be times when the media will take an adversarial role with your COB. This is much rarer than you might think. In the vast majority of cases, they are simply looking for a reasonable, plausible, supportable explanation for what you have said or done. The problems arise when your explanations are unreasonable, implausible and unsupportable. Or not forthcoming at all.

And they love a good fight. *Conflict* is what they feed on. Don't be an enabler.

Help them understand your COB. They don't have to be on your side, but don't make it easy for them to dislike you, to have a bias against you, even before you engage them.

This is not as easy as it sounds. Some reporters are belligerent, rude and disrespectful. They push and prod, goading their subjects into emotional answers, pushing them into corners and making the interview uncomfortable and difficult. They come into the interview with a bias and push their agenda hard.

Here's the good news – these reporters are a small minority. They get a lot of attention because of their aggressive style, but they do not represent the majority.

Advisors

When things are going badly for your COB, and they will, and you're sitting with your communications advisors to plan your communications strategy and prepare for a media encounter, tell them *everything*. Every sordid fact, every mistake, every miscalculation, every vulnerability. Treat your communications advisors like your lawyer. They need to know everything in order to help you prepare.

'Cause if you leave the bad stuff out, the advice you get will not be as complete as it needs to be. And when the bad stuff surfaces, and it will, you'll have lost the trust of the people who can help you a lot when you need it most.

Good communications advisors know who they can and cannot trust in their organization to give them the whole story. If they must deal with an unreliable colleague, they will double and triple check the info they get from this dubious internal source.

Good communications advisors also ask all the ugly, challenging, difficult questions that you do not want to face, because they know these are the same questions the media will ask and they want you to be prepared. Although these questions may be unappreciated at the time, they'll pay off when it counts the most.

Agenda

If you don't have an agenda heading into a media contact, you're missing the whole point. When the media call – or when you call them - an opportunity is created. Use it to your advantage.

Every media encounter must have an objective. What are you trying to say and why? To do this effectively, you have to have an agenda and be prepared to act on that agenda.

If you leave yourself to the mercy of the questions asked, you have given up control of the situation and deserve what you get – which, in most cases, will be unhappiness and an opportunity missed.

Aiding and Abetting

When a reporter calls and is pursuing a story in which your COB is involved, do your best to help them in a way that's advantageous to you.

And if there is background you can provide that involves other COBs – partner organizations, for example - provide them with the names and contact info for the appropriate people at that organization. The reporter will be grateful to you, and it will help strengthen your relationship with them. (And the second you hang up the phone with the reporter, you dial or text the person at the other organization to let them know the reporter's coming their way.)

Anger

Very, very rarely helpful.

There are a few occasions in which appearing aggravated or impatient may help, although these are uncommon.

90% of the challenge is to present yourself as a rational, believable professional, an expert in your field.

When you get angry, you give that all up. You look foolish, *plus* you hand control of the situation to the reporter.

Be cool.

Anticipation

How will you ever know what the reporter will ask you?

Well, you can ask them when they contact you. That works most of the time. You simply explain that you want to be well-prepared for the interview. They'll tell you.

If they won't tell you, you may not want to talk to them.

As well, always prepare to cover the basic questions reporters ask: Who? What? When? Where? Why? …and How much will it cost?

And take a moment to consider what other current situations or controversies in which your COB is involved. Just because the interview isn't about them doesn't mean the reporter won't bring them up. Be ready.

And when you consider those questions, do so from a reporter's perspective. Make them edgy and challenging, with a little editorial content thrown in. "Many people are unsatisfied with the clean-up you did on that site. You've had 6 months to do it and you still haven't met the minimum criteria. What's the problem? Why haven't you done a better job?"

We had worked very hard to stay close to a major issue, as our government minister was going to hold a significant news conference about the government's response to the issue.

We had tracked the media and public commentary and knew where the hot spots were. The minister knew what he wanted to say in each area.

His remarks had been carefully prepared to answer the most prominent questions around the issue.

And we had identified dozens of questions he would/could be asked on the various facets of the issue.

And for fun, we had created a list of the top 10 questions we thought the reporters would ask, based on our understanding of what we felt was important to them.

When the Q&A portion of the media conference started, they asked the first nine – in order! They got number 10 wrong.

It can be done. It's not that hard. It does require you to stop, put your interests aside and consider what their perspective will be.

Attribution (Not for)

There will be times when you'll want to provide reporters with background about your COB. This can be done in many ways. The best way is to sit and talk to them. And if you can provide accurate information, with access to deeper background through annual reports, business plans, etc., fine.

These conversations can be had on a "not for attribution" basis. This is simply background. It's not the place for opinions or speculation, it's simply information about your COB and the landscape in which it's working. So the conversation must be arranged on a "not for attribution" basis.

This is not the same as "off the record". The information that's being provided will be used in stories, it just won't be attributed to an individual. You will not be quoted.

You *are* responsible for the accuracy of the information, though. It's gotta be right.

Inaccurate information provided in these circumstances will damage the relationship significantly, especially if you're stupid enough to try to mislead a reporter in this process.

Availability

Good COBs that take their reputations seriously make themselves available to the media to answer questions about their operations and plans. They are accountable to their customers and the communities in which they operate.

Maintain a consistent level of availability, responding to media requests that are reasonable.

And make sure reporters know how to find you and the best way to get in touch – phone, email, text, carrier pigeon – whatever works.

That said, stay in your lane and do not speak or speculate about situations outside your domain. You will get pressure from media to speak on stories to which you may only have a tangential relationship – simply because you are available and the key figure in the issue isn't talking. Be very careful. When in doubt, decline.

B

Background (See also Patience)

As technology evolves and media outlets continue to downsize, you will encounter more and more general reporters who cover a wide variety of COBs. The chances of them knowing and understanding yours are small.

Be prepared to explain how your COB works, and the context in which it works – even if the reporter doesn't ask.

Misunderstandings the reporter may have, or assumptions they may make, will find their way into the story, through no malice on their part.

Lay a foundation of understanding and build on it.

It's time well spent.

Basics

When the media request arrives, there are things you must know before you agree to be part of the story.

Who are they and what media outlet do they represent?

Make a note of this for future reference.

What is the story about?

Don't be reluctant to probe this element.

Why are they calling you? What do they think you can contribute?

This may not be obvious. It will help determine the context of the interview and your level of involvement.

If there are aspects of the story that you simply cannot discuss for one reason or another (confidentiality, for example) explain this to the reporter NOW.

What is the reporter's deadline? In this digital age, it's most likely *now*, or as soon as they can get it together. That said, asking this question will indicate that you have some understanding and appreciation for their work. This helps build that good working relationship with them.

Does the reporter need background information on the story? If so, help them find what they need.

Brevity

Brevity is one of The Three "Ts": brevity, clarity and simplicity. Start with these three principles in mind, especially in your initial responses. There are usually plenty of opportunities to expand.

Long, rambling answers can be acceptable in long form stories, but for the most part, shorter, more concise points are much more useful. Expand from them, as needed, to make your points and deliver on your agenda.

Bridging

This is how you get from the question the reporter is asking to the answer you want to give. Not that you can ignore the question. Instead, listen for the *essence* of the question, the value it speaks to (integrity, safety, care for customers, etc.) and move from there to your agenda of telling your story and delivering your messages.

Examples:

"The primary focus in this situation is safety. At ABC Corporation, we have a strong commitment to safety. That's why we do safety audits every six months, which is more than government regulations require."

"You've raised the very important subject of quality control. We've instituted an extra layer of product quality tests to ensure our products are of the highest quality."

"What's most important here from our perspective, is fairness for our customers. We made a mistake and we're fixing it. That's why we're…"

"Let me reiterate why we've taken the steps we have, to address your point…"

"Your question raises a couple of issues. Let me deal with the most important one first…"

"What this whole situation is really about is…"

C

Changing Face of the Media

Media outlets are in the business of news gathering and dissemination. The same market and disruptive technological forces that face every other business also challenge them.

Over the past couple of decades, this has meant smaller staffs and fewer resources. There are many more generalists in the field than there used to be. Many more. As a result, you are quite likely to encounter a reporter who has little or no knowledge of your COB, and who's had virtually no time to do any research. Your COB is the story today, tomorrow they're covering a dog show.

As a result, you must be prepared to be patient, explain situations and issues clearly and to provide concise context and useful background information.

Clarity

This is one of "The Three Ts", along with *simplicity* and *brevity*.

To keep your answers clear, use simple words, avoid jargon and the temptation to show the world how smart you are. Be a real person.

Start with "The Three Ts", especially in your initial responses. There are usually plenty of opportunities to expand.

Clips

In an interview that's being done for a newscast, keep your answers crisp and brief. Five to eight seconds is fine.

On air, the reporter will provide background and context for the story. You are there to provide the face of your COB, or an exclamation point, or a presence. Long, rambling dissertations are difficult to edit, and do not serve your agenda.

Comment?

There will be times when a recorded interview will not be useful to you - a situation in which you may wish to provide a general comment, but not be a central figure in a story by providing a recorded interview. The subject may be too sensitive, or your COB's involvement may be so tangential that if you do a recorded interview, it will appear as if you are at the centre of the situation, when you are not.

You will be assuming a level of ownership of the issue that's not appropriate.

It is perfectly legitimate to decline a recorded interview for these reasons.

"As much as I'd like to help, this really isn't about us. This is a municipal story that only affects us slightly, so I'm going to leave it to them."

"This really is for the Mayor to speak to. I don't want us to take on more of a role than what's appropriate. Sorry I'm not in a position to be more helpful."

Always remember, while you will want to be helpful and accommodating to media people, your first loyalty must be to your COB. You are their face and voice.

Comments (Online)

Don't put any stock in the anonymous online comments that some media outlets allow their readers/viewers/listeners to post.

People with well-researched, thoughtful comments don't offer their opinions here.

These attacks can be mean, spiteful and personal.

If you are the person being quoted and now attacked, ignore them. I know this is very hard to do, because that's your name, your reputation and your COB that's under attack. Walk away. Reading them will not help you.

(But do have a communications advisor skim them to see if there are elements worthy of response or clarification.)

In most cases, the comments resort to personal attacks back and forth between the commenters fairly quickly.

Commitments

As you would in any relationship that's important to you, keep your commitments to reporters. If you say you'll be available at a given time and place, be there, on time and ready to go.

If you say you'll get answers and get back to them by a given hour, call them at that hour, even if it's to say you're still working on it. Or that there's nothing new on the situation.

Trust is a key element in any relationship and keeping your promises to reporters is one of the best ways to show why they should trust you.

Communication (Test of Effective)

Writing is the acid test of effective communication. If one person can write something down, pass it to another person and have that second person understand *exactly* what the writer meant. THAT is effective communication.

That's why it's important to write down objectives and answers to key questions. This way you get to stare at the words and phrases, dissect them, and discover whether they actually are conveying your meaning and serving your agenda.

Complaints

To maintain your good relations with reporters, contact them first if you think your COB's been hard done by by one of their stories. If you're not happy with the reception you get from the reporter, move up to the editor or news director. If you're still not satisfied, you may wish to pursue the issue with the Managing Editor or General Manager or owner. At all levels, though, you must be polite and respectful.

Do your homework – be prepared. You must be factual, not emotional.

When people get upset about how stories are portrayed by the media, the aggravation can usually be traced to these areas:

Factual Errors – Factual errors that appear in media reports must be corrected quickly because subsequent reports will be based on this information.

Tone – This is usually language-based. There is quite a difference between "declined" and "refused", between "criticized" and "blasted" and between "outbreak" and "epidemic". It can also be reflected in a photo that accompanies a story. Careful consideration should be given before raising a tone issue with a reporter or editor, due to the subjectivity involved.

Structure – The way a story is presented can create a bias. For example, a bias is apparent when a critic's viewpoint is reflected in the headline and the first ten paragraphs of a story, and the response to the criticism is buried or given little attention. Good reporters and editors are sensitive to this and you should get a reasonable response if you raise your concern respectfully.

Early in my career, I developed a reputation as someone who would call and aggressively challenge reporters over the slightest discrepancy in their stories. I was working in a government department that had a history of being unfairly maligned for many years and they were particularly sensitive about how they were portrayed in the media.

In retrospect, I could have and should have been more diplomatic. Then again, as years passed and I matured in my approach, it was much easier to loosen up than it would have been to tighten up.

That said, it's important that media people understand we're seeing what they report and we are willing to push back when we think it's appropriate.

Conflict

This is the media's bread and butter. It's when things go wrong that they're interested.

Don't expect them to come calling when things are fine – or even when you've done something terrific.

I worked in a major teaching hospital. In a slightly contentious conversation with a reporter, I pointed out, somewhat testily, that "Hey, we saved some people's lives here today." His response? "Hey, that's what you're supposed to do." Point taken. You will not get particular credit for doing things right. Don't go looking for it from the media.

Context

As part of your preparation, consider what else is happening in your COB, in your industry, or in your community that you may be asked about.

And consider whether it's to your advantage to even speak to any of the issues that may be raised that are outside the focus of the interview. If so, weigh in. If not, indicate that the topic is something you're happy to leave to others.

Control

In media situations, you enjoy much more control than you may think.

You control whether the interview even takes place.

You control your answers and the tone in which they're provided.

You control your attitude.

You do not control the reporter's questions, their attitude, or the story they create. Although, you can influence these elements through your own behaviour. The more reasonable, patient and co-operative you are, the more reasonable, patient and co-operative they will be. For the most part.

This is the point that so many people can't seem to get their head around. Fear of the media is based on the misconception that you are at their mercy. You are not.

Not that you don't have any responsibility to them, you do. You are responsible for keeping your commitments to them and to treat them with respect.

And to expect the same consideration in return.

A television reporter called and wanted to interview our CEO. Nothing specific, just the state of the COB in general. The CEO told me he wasn't interested in speaking to the media. That was my job. Plus, the reporter would not be specific about what aspect of this complex organization he wanted to ask about. The reporter did not want to talk to me, only the CEO. With the CEO's approval, I told the reporter it was me or nobody. The interview didn't happen. Relations with that one reporter were chilly for a while, but he came back around when he needed us later on for another story.

Corrections/Clarifications

These can be achieved by following the advice above in the Complaints section.

Digital stories are fairly easy to correct/clarify. On the other hand, corrections in print are usually quite unsatisfying. The front page mistake is often corrected in small print on lightly-read Page Two.

Responsible media outlets will admit their mistakes. Irresponsible ones won't care.

Creating your own Content

More and more COBs are creating their own media platforms and speaking directly to their audiences. They use video, several social media channels, even email to spread the good word.

Fine. Here's the issue, though. Everything they put out is sunshine and lollypops, and those platforms go silent when they're in a pickle.

Wrong. If you invest in various communication channels to your audiences, which should include traditional media outlets by the way, then use them when things are unhappy for you. In fact, this is exactly when those media channel investments can pay off. If you've used them well, you have developed a rapport with your audiences, you've built up some trust. Now, when things are dicey, enhance that trust by coming clean, telling the truth (as you see it), and explaining your side of the story and what you're doing to fix things.

If you shut these channels down when the clouds roll in, you will undermine their effectiveness and lose your audience. Plus, it will give the media another stick with which to hit you. And rightfully so.

Credibility

An audience will make virtually instantaneous judgements as to your credibility, even before you answer your first question. Yes, it's not fair, but such is the way of the world.

That's why your appearance must be credible, your answers must be credible and your message must not test the elasticity of the audience's imagination.

Working as the Public Affairs & Communications Director in a major teaching hospital, as you'd expect, our VP Medical was a doctor. When he did TV interviews, regardless of the topic, I would insist he put on his white examination coat, and string a stethoscope around his neck so he'd look the part. Worked every time.

Crisis and Opportunity

"Never let a good crisis go to waste."

While its origin is murky, this concept has been applied in many areas, from medicine to business to politics. Generally, it refers to the opportunities created to move an agenda forward that otherwise wouldn't exist.

The same applies in communications. And you don't need a four-alarm crisis. It's equally applicable in a run of the mill issue.

The opportunity is to showcase your COB. Even when you've messed up, or your COB's facing very public problems - see Tylenol, Boeing Dreamliner battery issue, Maple Leaf Foods, etc. Here's a chance to show how responsible you are in fixing your mistake, moving aggressively to protect your customers or the public and taking steps to ensure the problem's not repeated.

Of course, you have to take those aggressive steps. And communicate them effectively. Rarely does slamming the bunker door and hoping they all go away serve you well.

By the way, this will probably mean you'll need to put the dire warnings of your legal advisors in perspective. Do what you feel is the right thing. Then communicate that you're doing the right thing.

D

Deadlines

Always ask the reporter what sort of deadline they're working under. It shows you understand a little bit about what sort of pressure they may be facing. Again, it helps with the relationship.

That said, with most media operating in multiple formats, including online, often the deadline is as soon as the item can be prepared. In other words, the deadline is *now*.

If the reporter's deadline is unworkable for you, you are not under any obligation to turn your world inside out to accommodate it. If the request is unreasonable "We need your CEO on the phone in five minutes.", then the answer is no.

This is part of your control over the situation. Don't be afraid to use it. A reporter's deadline is not your deadline. Do what you can to help them, but never to your disadvantage.

Deafness

When you have said what you came to say at your media conference or scrum, this is what you must develop when it's time to pull the plug.

When you are finished saying what you came to say and have answered all the reasonable questions, you must physically remove yourself, ignoring the irrelevant questions being tossed at you as you leave.

At first, this will feel rude, like leaving a conversation when the other person still has something to say. It is not.

If you stop to re-engage, you are handing control of the situation back to the reporters. This usually ends badly.

Walk away. You've done what you came to do. You owe the media no more than what you've given. Leave.

A doctor at the hospital where I worked had been charged with murdering a patient. This drew national and international media interest. We, the hospital, got through the first 24 hours by issuing a statement. The media's main focus in that first day was the police and the doctor. On day two, they wanted a hospital representative, in the flesh.

To this point in my career, I'd never faced that many TV cameras or reporters.

Nervous? You bet. Well prepared? Yup.

And when the time came, when the key questions had been asked and answered and the energy in the room dropped, I thanked them, stood up, ignored the unimportant questions being lobbed my way, took two steps to the rear and stepped out of the board room and closed the door behind me. And exhaled.

That would be the beginning of a four month media odyssey as this story unfolded through the courts and through the hospital administration. A major learning process and defining experience for me, for which I am very grateful.

Delivery

In a video interview, delivery counts for about 85%, give or take.

If you *look* calm, knowledgeable and confident, you will be perceived as credible. The words you actually say are less important than the image you project. Not that you can spew gibberish. But the viewer will make an almost instantaneous judgement by looking at you, as to whether you can be trusted. *Then*, they will start listening.

In a radio interview, if you *sound* calm, knowledgeable and confident, you're 85% of the way toward representing your position well.

Radio can be a challenge. It's a "hot" medium, as the listener creates in their mind an image of the speaker, depending on what they hear. Have you ever met a radio announcer who looked just like your mental image of them? Me neither.

I've done lots of early morning radio news show interviews in my pyjamas, from my desk at home with notes in front of me. Much easier than live TV, believe me. In both cases, the huge value of preparation pays off.

Double-ender

This is a TV interview technique in which the subject of the interview - you - are not in the same room as the interviewer.

You get wired up by a technician, and you hear the questions from the interviewer through an earpiece. You give your answers looking directly into the camera.

Important considerations: Make sure you can hear the questions clearly. Remember that you are on camera before the questions actually start, so start looking smart before the questions start. Do not let your eyes wander from the camera - to the folks watching, you will look evasive and untrustworthy. The camera lens is the interviewer's face. Look them in the eye.

This can be a little unnerving the first time you do it. A little practice beforehand will be useful.

The first time I did a double-ender, I wasn't even in the same city as the interviewer. I sat in a darkened TV studio for what seemed like an hour before it was my time to go on. (It was a live interview.) It was really only about 10 minutes. I kept rolling key messages and my objectives over and over in my head. The key is to keep breathing, try to relax and remind yourself that you know way more about the subject than the person asking the questions.

E

Educating Reporters

Taking the time to explain how your COB works and the context in which it works, is always a good investment of time.

It also means you'll get better questions from reporters. Intelligent, knowledgeable questions are always easier to answer than uninformed, irrelevant questions. (That's because, with bad questions, you need to spend the first part of the answer politely explaining how the question is flawed and *then* provide an answer.)

Editorials

Pay attention to editorials in respected media outlets. Not everybody pays attention to them, although influencers and opinion leaders tend to.

If they're way off base, submit an op-ed, or ask for equal time.

Good media outlets that care about their integrity will provide the time/space.

Ego

Reporters have egos. In some cases, large ones. This can leave them vulnerable to flattery. Advantage you.

And some people being interviewed by the media have large egos. Advantage them.

Remember, it's not about you. It's about your COB and its audiences. They should be front and centre when planning your interactions with media.

Energy and Emotion

Don't be afraid to let the positive aspects of your personality shine through in an interview.

If you feel strongly about the topic - and you should if it's your COB - let that passion show through. Don't hide it. Demonstrate your conviction.

After I'd left the hospital, there was a major mass casualty incident. The hospital CEO, with whom I'd worked when she was a VP, stood in front of the TV cameras and brought professionalism, empathy and genuine caring to the moment. Not easy to do in the midst of a traumatic event. Although I wish I could, I take no credit for this. She was bringing her personality and heart to an awful situation. She reflected the level of caring that she'd helped nurture throughout the organization.

Engaging the Media

There are various ways of letting the media know you have something important to say.

From a straightforward media release, to an advisory, to a full on media briefing and levels in between.

It's important to choose the proper level of engagement. Skilled communications advisors will choose the right one at the right time.

Generally speaking...

A low level event that you'd like the media to be aware of warrants a Media Advisory – a very straightforward notice that something is happening at a given time and place, in which they may be interested, including contact information for someone who can provide more details and context.

A Media Release outlines what's happening, what it means and why it matters. It will often include quotes from participants and provides contacts for media follow up.

A Media Briefing provides explanations of important situations of significant interest. These involve a speaker or speakers making opening statements, Q & A from reporters and perhaps some one-on-one interviews. In some cases, a media tour of a facility can be part of the briefing.

Choose wisely. Do not abuse the relationship. (See Newsworthy)

Equal Treatment

You do not owe every media outlet equal treatment.

If a media outlet that has treated you fairly over time has the foresight to see something coming and is calling you regularly to see when it's going to happen, there is no issue in giving them a heads-up as to when the story they've been chasing is about to break.

It's part of managing the relationship.

They treat you fairly, you give them a break. You needn't give them everything. Save some good stuff for the announcement.

If they have treated you badly in the past, they can wait and get the news with everyone else.

Caveat: This applies to general media announcements. There will be situations around publicly-traded companies, statements in legislative assemblies, or concerning legal matters, when no one gets a break, for good reasons - it's imprudent, against the rules of the institution or illegal.

I have done this several times, to good effect. From my perspective, the reporter got the reward they had earned, and good on them for it.

Errors (Omission, Commission)

When a COB gets upset about how stories are portrayed in the media, the aggravation can usually be traced to these areas:

1. **Factual Errors** – Factual errors that appear in media reports must be corrected quickly because subsequent reports will be based on this information.

2. **Tone** – This is usually language-based. There is quite a difference between "declined" and "refused", between "criticized" and "blasted" and between "outbreak" and "epidemic". Careful consideration should be given before raising a tone issue with a reporter or editor, due to the subjectivity involved.

3. **Structure** – The way a story is presented can create a bias. For example, in a print story, a bias is apparent when a critic's viewpoint is reflected in the headline and the first ten paragraphs of a story, and the response to the criticism is buried or given little attention. Good reporters and editors are sensitive to this.

When seeking a clarification or correction, it's appropriate to start with the reporter. If you're not happy with the reception you get, move up to the editor or news director. If you're still not satisfied, you may wish to pursue the issue with the Managing Editor or General Manager. At all levels, though, you must be polite and respectful.

Do your homework – be prepared. You must be factual, not emotional.

Examples

Look for relevant examples or analogies you can use to help make a complex matter simpler and more understandable for the audience.

Be very careful, though, not to use an example that excludes relevant information.

Exhaustion

When you find yourself on a full-blown crisis, a media storm that goes on for days, keep an eye on your media relations/communications people.

Stress and fatigue exhaust even the strongest, best people. Call in the cavalry. Get some back up. They will resist, but it must be done.

For starters, they *look* exhausted on TV, and that hurts your credibility.

And they make poor decisions.

Make your lead people rest, and then bring them back for another round.

At the airport, we had a commercial airliner crash in the middle of the night, on the weekend, in a blizzard. Very fortunately, none of the 138 passengers and crew on the plane was seriously injured. I operated on very little sleep for several days. I was slow to call in the help we needed. In fact, it was a colleague who made the suggestion. I was so wrapped up in what we were doing, it simply didn't occur to me. We had a strong team and we were handling things. But he was right. The fact was, I was becoming less effective because I was exhausted. We got help. Thank goodness.

Exit Strategy

In a media conference, ensure that your speaker or speakers - the person or persons at the podium or head table - have an easy exit from the room. This way, when they are finished saying what they came to say and have answered all the reasonable questions, they can take their leave, without having to wade through the media people and be peppered with questions on the way by. That never works well, as it appears they are avoiding questions. (It looks that way because that's what they are doing.)

Remember, this is *after* they have answered all the reasonable questions.

In every media conference or scrum, there will arrive a time when all the basic questions have been answered and the reporters will start picking at the edges of the situation. The speakers have said what they came to say, the energy in the room drops, the questions start getting a little silly. It's time to go. A firm, polite "Thank you very much." And the speakers are up and gone, oblivious to the questions being lobbed at them. (See Deafness)

Experience

The best teacher.

If you're encountering the media on a regular basis, this is a big advantage in that you can build a rapport, develop the relationship, educate them as to where the boundaries are, and demonstrate your willingness to help them do their job.

Caution: If you are dealing with reporters on a regular basis, be careful. Familiarity can breed contempt, in both directions. You may think you don't need to prepare as diligently and that may be true in some cases. However, if you treat these encounters too casually, it will burn you at some point. Remember, just because they are friendly doesn't mean they're your friends.

It's much tougher if you're only doing a few interviews a year. That's when preparation and practice are critical.

Just because they are friendly doesn't mean they're your friends.

A high profile national TV investigative reporter called and wanted to interview the minister of justice for whom I was working. We were involved in a major situation and she was interested in talking to him about it. She was friendly and flattering. He agreed to do the interview.

A few days later, she showed up at his office. We had worked hard to get him ready. He was a good person in a tough spot.

In any event, because they had just one camera to work with, she proposed that she'd interview the minister, with the camera on him, and then she'd repeat the questions, with the camera on her. Fine.

There were just four of us in his office – minister, reporter, cameraman and me.

So, with the camera on him, she started asking questions – tough, pointed, very challenging questions posed in provocative ways. She really went after him.

He did his best, although her aggressive approach was a bit much for him at points and his answers were in many cases defensive and incomplete.

When the inquisition ended, she thanked him for his time.

A little rattled, he left the office, while she prepared to repeat the questions to be taped for the broadcast.

I watched as she recorded her questions. But this time around, her tone was polite, deferential and empathetic. The sharp, aggressive edge to her initial questions was nowhere to be seen.

As they packed up, I mentioned to her this rather drastic change in tone.

"That's the way we do it," she said on her way out the door.

Needless to say, when the interview was aired on national TV a week later, there she was, kind and empathetic with her questions and the minister looking defensive and shaken.

I have often wondered what, if anything, I could have said or done to change that outcome. Would it have mattered if I'd objected *to the tone of the taped questions? I don't know. I do know that I never looked at this award-winning national news personality the same again. Not that she'd care.*

Just because they are friendly doesn't mean they're your friends.

Lesson learned.

F

Facts

Check them, then check them again.

Getting the facts wrong undermines your credibility. Quickly.

Get them. Know them. Use them to support your Key Message.

Fairness

One of the key qualities your COB can reasonably expect from your encounters with the media is *fairness*. Did they get the facts right? Were they even-handed in their presentation of the story? Was there any apparent bias?

There is no such thing as objectivity. Reporters bring a set of biases to every story they cover. They are human, after all. They like some things and don't like others. They particularly don't like people who lie to them and treat them badly. Then again, *we* don't like people who lie to us and treat us badly.

Reporters may like you, which can be useful. Or they may not like you, which can be detrimental to your COB. A great deal of their attitude is based on how you treat them. The correlation is simple and direct – treat them badly, they will go out of their way to make trouble for you; treat them well and they will at least listen to you explain yourself after you've done something stupid.

It's a *relationship*. Do your part.

But please, never expect them to be completely objective. You'll be disappointed every time.

"Found" Information

When a media outlet invests time and money to find information, they tend to use it, even if it's not terribly important.

If your COB is the object of that information, one of your key tasks is to put that information into its proper context, to show that it's not important or particularly relevant, and instead, provide information that *is* important in that situation. In other words, seek out the opportunity this media inquiry provides and use it to your advantage.

"Given" information, on the other hand, has less value because everyone has it. Big deal.

I have been involved with situations in which the institutions where I worked were facing deadlines to provide embarrassing or damaging information to a media outlet or critic under freedom of information rules. In several cases, we released the information widely just before being required to provide it to the organization that requested it. There are at least two advantages to this – firstly, it allowed us to manage the information release and frame the information in a less damaging light; and secondly, since everyone had the information, it's far less valuable. Yes, it's still damaging, but much less so.

The situation we faced was, "Yes, we're going to get whacked in the head for this, but how much is it going to hurt?" We were trying to lessen the damage.

Friends

Earlier, you were reminded – "Remember, just because they are friendly doesn't mean they're your friends."

But, what if they *are* your friends, or your neighbours?

A couple of things:

Good reporters are very curious people, and usually great talkers. That chat over the backyard fence or at the barbeque could be the germ of a story. As a general rule, don't talk about anything, especially your COB that you aren't comfortable having them pursue professionally.

Try to keep the professional boundaries between you clear and intact.

Don't take it personally if they try to use your friendship to get some inside information about your COB. Asking questions and sniffing around things is what they do. Just as they shouldn't take it personally if you pitch them on a story about some good stuff your COB is up to.

Full Disclosure

When you're in trouble, tell your communications advisors EVERYTHING, like you would your lawyer. They need the full picture to give you their best advice.

G

Guarantees

As in, there are none.

Things can and do go wrong at either end of a media encounter. Most often, these are not the result of any malicious intent by either of the parties involved. This is why the development of a solid relationship with media people is so important.

As in any relationship, misunderstandings can happen. When they do, move quickly to straighten things out and get the relationship back on solid ground.

Goal

You must have a goal, an objective every time you do a media interview.

All of the decisions you control – from the timing and location of the interview, to the answers you give and the tone with which you give them - must serve to achieve that goal.

And if it's anything more than a routine media chat, write the goal down. Make sure it's the most effective for your COB in these circumstances.

Grammar

If you use bad grammar in a media interview, you might as well have spinach in your teeth on TV. Credibility damaged.

H

Heart

Have one.

Empathy and gratitude show you're a real person who cares about the people involved in whatever situation you're talking about.

Your job is to answer the questions accurately and in a way that demonstrates you care. (The best way to do this is to actually care.)

Honesty

Do I really have to tell you to never lie to a reporter in an interview?

Okay, I will. NEVER lie to a reporter in an interview.

Never make stuff up. Never speculate about what might happen.

The truth will always present itself, probably at the worst possible moment.

Keep your life simple. Tell the truth. The whole truth.

And there was one time I didn't. From my perspective, I felt I couldn't. And I bore the reporter's wrath.

An enterprising print reporter, with whom I had a solid working relationship over some years, called my justice department office late one afternoon and directed me to a particular section of the Criminal Code. He asked me to read it and consider it in relation to a decision the department had made with regard to a particular judge. I read it, and I believe my response to the reporter was "Yikes". Certainly, on the face of it, it appeared the justice minister may have broken the law. I told him I'd call him back. He asked me if any other reporter had called about this, and I told him no. He said he did not intend to write the story for the next day's paper. He wanted to see how it was going to play out, and he figured he could afford to wait, as no one else was on it.

I immediately engaged the deputy minister, who sought out the minister and senior lawyers in the department to get their perspective on the situation. These discussions lasted into the evening.

As you would expect, my office phone rang early the next morning. (This was pre-voice mail, cell phone, email, or text.) It was the enterprising reporter, looking for an update.

The fact was the minister had made the decision to follow the proper legal protocol and refer the matter to the chief of police, and let him decide whether a charge was warranted. The letter was being drafted and the plan was that it would be delivered that morning. And since our House of Assembly was in session, the minister would make a statement to this effect when the House sat at noon. That statement was being drafted. By me.

So, what did I tell the enterprising reporter? I told him we were still considering what he'd brought to our attention and that we hadn't reached any firm decisions. The truth? No. Was I in a position to tell him the truth? I sure didn't think so. The letter had yet to be sent. That decision could change. The minister's statement in the house had yet to be made. That decision could change.

The enterprising reporter called several times that morning, each time a little more agitated than the time before. Each time he would ask if any other reporter called about the matter. They had not and I told him so.

The letter to the chief of police was delivered that morning. At noon, we went to the House of Assembly where, shortly after proceedings began, the minister rose and read the statement that outlined the whole situation.

Because the enterprising reporter was not present – he didn't cover the House of Assembly, one of his colleagues did – he wasn't there when the whole world was let in on the story he'd uncovered.

I knew it was just a matter of time before he tracked me down – again, this was pre-cell phone, text, etc. I was back at the office a couple of hours later when his call came. As you'd expect, he was very upset. I'd lied to him and blown this great story right out from under him. I didn't argue with him, because he was right. I'd done exactly that. I did point out, though, that my loyalty had to be to the minister and the department. He was going to come second on that list every time. I told him I regretted what had happened, although I would do the same thing tomorrow, if the circumstances warranted.

He was mad at me. Rightfully so.

He didn't call me for a while. Understandable.

While he understood why things unfolded as they had, he certainly didn't like it. And I didn't blame him.

In the long run, I don't think he ever forgave me completely, but the relationship wasn't irreparably damaged and things got back to normal shortly thereafter.

Sometimes doing the right thing and telling the truth in a particular moment can be mutually exclusive.

I

Interview

A one-on-one media interview is a conversation – a formal conversation.

In most cases, the interviewer asks a question, the interviewee is then given the opportunity to respond. (Do not abuse this opportunity by running on and on. Keep your responses clear, simple and fairly brief.)

The interviewer may interrupt, if the answers being given are too far off topic or are factually questionable. Otherwise, the interviewee has the chance to answer and explain.

It's important that you have an agenda for your answers. Anticipate the questions. Discern the values that apply. Get the facts to support your position. Connect the values to the facts. Connect the questions you anticipate to the messages you want to deliver.

Manage the situation as best you can, because you cannot control it.

Introduction (Your)

As with any public appearance, make sure you control the way you are introduced. If you're a corporate communications person, you may be referred to as a "spokesperson". Fine. If you're not, ensure your title is accurate and that any pertinent background information is included.

Don't be shy about this. Give it to the media outlet.

Example: "Speaking with us today is Bill Jones, the Vice President, Operations with Acme. Mr. Jones has been with the firm for 18 years and has seen these situations several times in his career…"

Issue versus Crisis

Did anyone die? Did anyone get wiped out financially? Reputationally?

If so, it's a crisis. All hands on deck.

Otherwise, it's an issue. Manage it and move on.

J

Jargon (Use of)

As a general rule, don't use jargon or industry-speak. These terms and acronyms simply confuse your audience.

Speak in plain, concrete language.

Remember – if your audience doesn't understand what you're saying and therefore can't use or relate to the information you're providing, you're not communicating effectively.

K

Key Messages

Key messages are points that you continuously stress to support your position and the values on which your position is based. (Others may disagree with your position, but the values you bring to bear should be unassailable.)

Identify one or two key messages – not 17 – and keep your answers focused on them.

Effective key messages support your COB's values. They address anticipated objections and accentuate the positive elements of situations. They are also rooted in the essence of the issue itself.

Key messages are not effective if they are simply facts you hope the media assemble correctly to convey your message. Key messages must be values-based and supported by facts. Become very familiar with them and practice using them out loud.

To repeat - Facts are *not* key messages. Facts are speaking points. Facts are used to support the values and principles that are the key messages.

Your job is to deliver the key message and then support it with the relevant facts.

Know the Audience

Different media outlets have different audiences.

Some audiences are sophisticated and knowledgeable. Some are not.

Be prepared for the difference.

Sophisticated and knowledgeable? Your answers and comments can be more elegant and obtuse.

Not so much? Keep it simple and obvious.

If in doubt, default to simple and obvious.

Know Your Stuff

To be effective for your COB in responding to the media, you've got to really know your stuff. You are the domain expert and you need to use that expertise to your advantage.

First off, you need to know and understand the facts of the matter - facts that have been checked and double checked. (Believe me, you don't want the follow up story to be that you got a central piece of information wrong.)

Secondly, you need to understand the emotion of the situation and respond accordingly. It's OK to show you care. Being cold and dealing with "just the facts" isn't enough. People respond to other people, not message machines.

Lastly, go over and over the material – out loud – to weed out poor choices of words or jargon the audience won't get, and to master the material and its presentation.

This level of preparation will be invaluable when the lights come on, and your nerves are a bit jangled. In other words, your delivery level will tend to drop when it's show time versus the run through you did in the familiar surroundings of your office or boardroom.

Be prepared.

I cannot stress this too much.

Each and every time that I've gotten myself into trouble in an interview, it's because I wasn't sufficiently prepared. It's a sinking feeling, standing in front of a TV camera and realizing mid-interview that you were just a little too nonchalant in getting ready. If you're lucky, you can get through it, usually using "process answers" (describing the process in detail, but not substance). If not, it means getting the substantive answers and following up with the reporter.

L

Language (Vocabulary)

The actual words that you use to answer the questions will set a tone that will help persuade others to your COB's position. Therefore, it's important to choose the right words that convey your position accurately and advantageously.

As a general rule, avoid negatives.

And do not repeat negatives the reporter uses in a question.

"Are you a crook"?

"No, I'm not a crook."

What people hear are the words "I'm" and "crook" in the same sentence coming out of your mouth.

Here are some simple examples of words and phrases you can substitute that will emit a more positive attitude on your part:

Negative	Neutral/Positive
disagree	see the situation differently
but	at the same time, although, and
spend	invest
problems	challenges

There are also phrases that you can use that draw the reporter toward your viewpoint that includes them in reasonable thinking. Here's an example: "As I'm sure you will appreciate…"

When you follow this phrase with a reasonable statement of your position, or the limits of your situation, it pulls the listener in and, at the same time, demonstrates the reasonableness of your position.

Here's an example:

"Although we face competing pressures, as I'm sure you will appreciate, our number one priority is the safety of our customers and their families. So, we have halted production, recalled all the affected products and we're co-operating with the authorities to ensure we find the root cause of the problem."

Legal Advice

In a litigious or potentially litigious situation, the legal advice most COBs receive is to say nothing. And from the legal perspective, this is reasonable.

That said, the legal perspective is only one of several that will come into play when executives are deciding what, if anything, to say and when and how to say it.

If your COB has a well-earned reputation for being accountable to the world around it, consideration must be given to the potential reputational damage that will be inflicted by suddenly adopting a bunker mentality and clamming up.

The useful balance between a COB's legal and communications consideration can be a high-wire balancing act.

Another challenging element is the time it takes to have communications vetted through the legal filter. Having lawyers who understand the need for prompt consideration of communication issues is very useful.

My best advice is to stay true to your COB's values and make your communications decisions based on them, even if it creates some legal vulnerability.

Legs

You can tell if a media story is going to be an issue for you when it has "legs". Those "legs" present themselves in a couple of ways.

For example, when other media outlets beyond the originators of the story pick it up and start to explore its various angles. (Media outlets are loathe to simply repeat what others, often their competitors, have already reported. So they'll tend to get creative and try to come at the story from new angles.) As a result, the story starts to spread out and starts to pull in elements outside the original story. This is not good for a couple of reasons. The essence of the story gets lost, plus what was a one-day wonder becomes a running saga, with tentacles that reach into areas of your COB that are irrelevant. But the beast must be fed and unimportant details will take on new significance as stories get padded and fluffed up.

A story shows its legs when media outlets editorialize on it and your COB.

When a story has legitimate legs, dig in and deal with it. Stand up, answer the questions honestly and properly and the story will fade. Don't get all defensive. That will tend to prolong the story and damage your relationship with reporters. Be patient. And be as tenacious in answering questions as they are in asking them.

The challenging stories are those that don't deserve their legs, but get them anyway, because of the novelty of the story, or because it's a slow news day, or because a media outlet really does have it out for you and here's their chance. Again, be patient and do your best not to prolong the agony by being indignant and self-righteous.

Lies

Don't tell them.

And don't make things up. If you don't know the answer, commit to getting it. Better to look unprepared than deceitful.

On more than one occasion, I witnessed government policy being invented on the spot, as an ill-prepared minister stumbled through the answer to a media question.

The standing wry joke in some departments was that they'd watch the proceedings of the House of Assembly on TV to see what new policies they'd be implementing.

Listen

Listen carefully to the premise of the media call you are managing. Listen for the accuracy of the premise and the background information from which the reporter is operating.

If the reporter is working under a misapprehension, get it straightened out NOW. Never assume they know and understand the situation they're calling about. Take time right up front to ensure the facts of the matter and the context in which they are operating is accurate.

Establishing facts and context early will save time and prevent errors in the story they produce. And the good reporters will appreciate it.

Long Form Interview

Lots of background, lots of context.

Even though these can take the form of several long interviews, it still means you need to prepare your agenda and drive that agenda. It just means you'll have more opportunities to hit the themes and key messages you want to promote.

The other element to be conscious of is the development of a familiarity with the reporter, which may lead you to say things you later regret. Yes, the Stockholm Syndrome. Be wary. They may be friendly, but unless you are paying them to write this story about you and your COB, they are not your friends.

Luck

Never underestimate what some good old luck can do to help your cause.

For example – you've made a mistake, a pretty good one. Although you are doing and saying all the right things, apologizing to those affected, taking steps to make things right and outlining how you will prevent this from happening again, the bare fact remains that you messed up and in a fairly public way.

And then along comes a much better, bigger, story. Suddenly, you're on page 10, or way down the online or evening news line-up and hardly anyone notices.

You got lucky. You can't count on it, but when it happens, it's a beautiful thing.

Working in the justice system, we'd messed up and I'd done a whole round of media interviews through the day explaining, as best I could, what had happened and what we were doing to fix it. We were going to get whacked. That evening, there was a major train derailment outside the city. Front page news. Dominated the media. Our gaffe was relegated way down the media's ladder, small story.

Luck. You can't live on it, but when it rolls your way, say thank you and move on.

M

Managing Expectations

Manage the media's expectations. If you have to say no to an element of the situation, access to the CEO, for example - say it early. Don't waste their time and keep them hanging.

Media

What used to be the bailiwick of a few has become democratized, for better or for worse. Media is everywhere, with virtually everyone creating content all the time.

So be careful out there. Privacy is becoming increasingly scarce.

Media Conference

A media conference or briefing provides explanations of important situations of significant interest. These involve a speaker or speakers making opening statements on behalf of your COB, questions from reporters and perhaps some one-on-one interviews when the formal conference is over. In some cases, a Media Tour of a facility can be part of the briefing.

Ensure that in your speaker's opening remarks the basic questions surrounding the situation are covered. (Who? What? When? Where? Why? How much will it cost? Who will pay?)

That won't prevent them from being asked again in the Q&A, but it provides you with a basis from which to elaborate.

Media Relations

It's a relationship. You need them. They need you. Therein lie the opportunities for you.

Monitoring

Pay attention to what's being said about your COB. But don't get obsessive about it. Remember, you can't control it, you can only influence it. And that's if you're good at it.

Look for the trend, not the one-off mention.

At the same time, correct factual inaccuracies ASAP. Future stories are built on these and so it's in your best interest to set the record straight right away.

Multiple Interviews (Same day, Same topic)

In a perfect world, you'd simply bring all the relevant media together, give your position and answer the questions. When that doesn't happen, you may find yourself giving several interviews on a particular situation in the run of a day.

The challenge in these situations is to offer the same information to each successive reporter. Be aware of the natural tendency to elaborate in each subsequent interview.

And although you may be bored by hearing yourself give the same answers, using the same examples over and over, it's important that you be consistent.

When I was working at a major airport, we had a bizarre incident in which a passenger let their cat out of its carrying case in the passenger compartment prior to takeoff. The cat took off, ran into the cockpit and got itself down between some panels into the nose of the plane into the wiring for the aircraft's electronics.

The flight was delayed for a couple of hours, as aircraft maintenance people had to remove the panels in the cockpit to extricate the cat.

Word got out on social media, as it was happening.

When the story hit the media, I got calls from around the world about "the cat in the cockpit". I must have done a dozen or more interviews and told the same story over and over. Believe me, it got tiresome very quickly.

An interesting sidebar to this situation was that the media were all quite concerned about the cat. They didn't care about the 150 people whose flight was eventually cancelled and whose travel plans that morning were completely disrupted. Nor did they care about the airline whose schedule for that aircraft that day went out the window.

N

Newsworthy

Despite what you may think inside your COB, not everything you do is worthy of a full on media barrage.

In managing your relationship with the media, it's important to pick your spots, so that when you do ask for their attention, it's worth their while to give it to you.

A flood of media releases and constantly clamouring for their attention makes you the needy one in the relationship. We're trying for a grown-up relationship in which both parties respect each other and understand that when something important happens, you'll be in touch.

"No Comment"

NEVER utter these two words. I mean, NEVER.

They are media code for "I'm guilty and my COB is guilty of all the awful things our opponents and critics are saying. We are bad people and no one should trust us now or ever again."

If you do not wish to comment on a situation at a given moment, there are many ways to speak and provide no comment without saying those two awful words.

Keep in mind, these are situation-dependent.

For example:

"This situation is evolving rapidly. We are still gathering information and we'll be in a position to speak to it more fully soon."*

"This situation does not involve us directly, and while we are concerned, we will leave direct comments to those who are dealing with it."

"Our thoughts are with those involved in this very difficult situation. That said, we have nothing to add at this time. If and when that changes, we'll be in touch."

* In this situation, you have a made a commitment to speak to the situation at some point. You must keep this promise. This statement buys you a little time. It does not remove you from the situation.

Nuance

For the most part, shades of meaning, subtleties and nuance are lost on reporters. For the most part, they will see the broad strokes of a story, but struggle to express fine elements within it.

What this means for you is that you will have more success when you express large, broad ideas than you will if you try to be too cute or introduce elegant shades of meaning.

Clear. Simple. Brief.

These elements work best.

Numbers

Make sure that any numbers you use in an interview have been thoroughly vetted and verified and the sources of those numbers are solid.

For some reason that a psychologist may be able to explain, numbers tend to stick in people's minds, regardless of whether they are accurate.

Your critics may introduce numbers that are wrong. You will have to work diligently to unseat those numbers and replace them with the right ones.

I have had several bad experiences on this front. Here's one: My city was in an international bidding process for a major sporting event. It was going to be expensive – manageable in our estimation, but pricey. The issue was that the exact cost was simply unknown. The elements were still being put together and we simply did not know the final price tag.

In response to pressure, a number purporting to be the total cost got floated and stuck. The problem was, the number was far below what the actual cost was going to be.

No matter how many times I explained this was a "preliminary estimate", the number stuck and we never got past it.

When the real number became apparent months later, the government funders succumbed to the public heat and our city withdrew from the bidding process.

O

Objectivity (and Unicorns)

Objectivity is a myth.

Reporters are human beings and they bring a set of biases to every story they cover. They like some things and don't like others. They particularly don't like people who lie to them and treat them badly.

The two qualities that you can reasonably expect from your encounters with the media are *accuracy* and *fairness*. Did they get the facts right? Were they fair in their presentation of the story? Was there an apparent bias?

"Off the Record"

There is no such thing as "off the record". Everything you do and say in the presence of the reporter is fair game for them to use.

If a reporter asks you something "off the record", stick to your planned responses and do not be drawn into such a discussion. You're on dangerous ground. There is very little upside for you.

And never *offer* a comment "off the record". The reporter may respect your confidence in the short term, but will likely be unable to resist the temptation in the long term.

Keep your life simple, and stay "on the record".

Yes, I admit it, I have gone "off the record" with reporters I know and trust. And, to the best of my knowledge, it has not hurt me, or the COB for which I was working.

In one particular instance, it helped my COB a great deal. Once. In decades.

(I'd love to tell you the story, "off the record". It's a doozy. But the people involved are good friends and they're still around and it wouldn't be fair to them. Maybe some other time.)

On the Record

Everything you do and say in the presence of a reporter is "on the record".

That's why you prepare so diligently. That's why, when and where the interview takes place are important factors.

When I worked at a major hospital, during the run up to major labour negotiations, we were under a fair bit of pressure. We were dealing with a particularly skilled reporter, who used a classic passive/aggressive approach - very understanding and empathetic one minute, but ready to skewer you with a "gotcha" question the next. He was a master at the conversation that seemed quite casual, but he was forever sniffing at the edges of the story, looking for weaknesses and angles to pursue. When he came to do an interview with us, our basic rule was that we could exhale and relax an hour after he left the property.

P

Paranoia (Healthy)

Check, double check and if needs be, triple check.

What can go wrong?

Where are the traps?

How are you going to handle them?

Details, details and more details.

Cover them off to raise your confidence level.

Cover them off to be fully prepared.

Failing to prepare is preparing to fail. (Unoriginal, but true.)

Patience

Depending on how knowledgeable and prepared the reporter is, you will either get thoughtful questions or stupid questions.

Be patient with the latter. They are an opportunity to educate the reporter and the world about your COB and how wonderful it is.

Person

As in, speak like a real one, versus one imitating a person being interviewed.

Be the best version of yourself you can. Talk *to* people, not *at* them.

People forgive people when they apologize for making a mistake.

They don't forgive soulless robots.

I was planning to cite an example of a company CEO going through the motions of an apology after his/her company messed up and hurt/killed people. But we've all seen it too often. Cold, meaningless words, delivered without conviction. Worse than saying nothing.

Permanence

Stuff stays around forever. So if you don't want to see it, hear it or read it forever, don't say it or do it.

Personality

Don't be afraid to let the positive aspects of your personality shine through in an interview.

If you feel strongly about what you're speaking on, let that passion show through.

Demonstrate your conviction about the subject at hand.

Pitch and Pace (and Tone)

You manage the emphasis you give to certain points by varying the tone, pitch and pace of your voice.

Lists and background information can be well delivered at a moderate pace.

Slow down when delivering your key message. Give it the emphasis it deserves.

Practice

Practice your answers OUT LOUD. Rehearse.

You do not want the actual interview to be the first time you hear yourself giving an answer. By practicing out loud, you get comfortable with the words you'll be using, and how you intend to frame your key messages and how you plan to bridge from the questions to your answers, to deliver on your agenda.

You will find this very awkward at first. Believe me, it's not as awkward as watching yourself stumble and stammer on TV.

Press

Could we please move on to "media"? Thank you.

There are fewer and fewer presses in the world every year.

Preparation (General)

To prepare properly, ensure you understand basic information, such as:

1. What is the reporter's name and what media outlet do they represent? Make a note of this for future reference. Make sure you know exactly who you are talking to. Are they the reporter, editor or producer?

   On a related note, make sure you know the perspective of this media outlet as it pertains to your company, your industry. That perspective will colour the questions you get and the attitude the interviewer brings to the situation. It can also affect whether you agree to the interview in the first place. This is where the knowledge and experience of your communications advisor comes into play. Don't have one? Then an investment in some professional communications/public affairs advice is in order. You wouldn't go to court without legal advice. Don't walk into the court of public opinion without communications advice.

2. What is the story about? Really. Don't be reluctant to probe this element. The context of the interview is very important.

   If there are aspects of the story that you simply cannot discuss for one reason or another (confidentiality, for example) explain this to the reporter NOW.

3. What is the reporter's deadline? Now? Today? This week? Longer? Asking this question indicates that you have some understanding and appreciation for their work. This helps build a good working relationship with them.

4. Does the reporter need background information on the story? If so, help them find what they need.

5. Determine the interview location. If it's in your office – not recommended - remove any sensitive material. If it's in a TV or radio studio, ensure you know the exact location and leave adequate time to get there so as not to be rushed.

If the interview is outdoors, make sure you know what's going on around you.

Preparation (Specific)

First:

Anticipate questions about the story at hand. (Who? What? When? Where? Why? How much? Who's paying?)

Plus, consider any spin-off issues the reporter may ask you about? What else is going on at your COB or in your industry that you may be questioned about?

And if you're in a news conference situation, be sure to answer the key anticipated questions in your opening remarks.

Next:

Decide on the 1 or 2 values-based key messages you wish to deliver. These become your agenda for the interview. Your key points must address the main elements of the story and the reporter's concerns. They cannot be unrelated or overly evasive.

Gather the necessary background information. These are the facts that support the values that are the basis for the key messages. Ensure the information you are using is current and accurate.

Develop "bridges" (see Bridging) between the questions you expect and the key messages you wish to deliver. Find the connections that move you from the reporter's question to your key message and the facts that support that message.

Decide what information you will provide voluntarily ("given") and what you will wait to be asked ("found"). If there are subjects you would rather not discuss during the interview, but that you may be asked about, prepare for those questions.

Finally:

Practice. Out loud. Take the questions. Test drive your answers. Adjust as required. Rehearse the whole situation to gain confidence in the strength of your position.

Print

Reading that awful media report in the newspaper, or online, over and over just makes you feel worse.

If you can repair some of the damage, do it.

If you can't, move on. Yes, it's painful, although rarely fatal.

And you'll run into lots of people who didn't even see it.

Proactive versus Reactive

There will be times when you'll want to be first in market with your position. For example, there is an issue brewing with your COB. You know that, at some point in the not too distant future, there will be media interest. And your opponents/competitors/critics will be on the hunt.

In this case, there is a significant advantage to get your message out first. There is great value in having that first, clean shot. You get to frame the issue in a manner advantageous to you. You get to frame the context and tell the world how you have been managing the situation and how you'll be managing it in the future.

Your critics will be in a reactive mode, having to try to refute what you've said.

Being first in market doesn't mean they won't take shots at you. It does mean that you have the opportunity to set the framework and context of the issue. A nice advantage.

If you wait, *you* will then be on the defensive, having to refute their claims against you. And unless they are way off in their attack on you, you're in a hole and will have to work that much harder to get out.

CAUTION – if you decide to take this first, clean shot, make sure you don't conveniently omit key elements of the story because they don't fit your objective. Resist the temptation to "spin" things your way. Your critics will hammer you for it and rightfully so. Give the full story. If you don't, you could be worse off than when you started.

Q

Questions

DO NOT LET THE QUESTION DICTATE THE ANSWER!!

You are not obliged to be confined by the question. The question is your invitation to speak.

Bridge from the question to your key message.

This is one of the ways you exert the control you have over the interview.

You have 100% control over the answer you give and the tone you use in giving it. If you limit yourself to the questions you are asked, you give up that control and allow the interviewer to set the agenda.

When you prepare well, you anticipate questions. You construct answers that help you meet your objective for the interview.

To be clear, if the question is a pitch right in over the plate, take a good swing.

But if the question is a sucker pitch, well outside the strike zone, bridge to your key message and deliver it.

Communications advisor: "Boss, why didn't you talk about all the wonderful things we're doing to help disadvantaged youth get jobs and experience in our 'Building for Tomorrow' Program?"

Boss: "They didn't ask me."

Communications Advisor (to self): "Deliver me from this idiot."

R

Radio

Radio is a "hot" medium, in that the listener constructs a mental picture of you from the sound and tone of your voice and the vocabulary you choose.

(…and from the introduction the host gives. You can influence that. See Introduction.)

In a radio interview, the tone and pitch of your voice and the pace at which you speak drive the listeners' perception and whether they grant you credibility.

This is where practice comes in. Out loud practice.

Nervous people tend to speak quickly. Their vocal cords tighten and their voices are higher than their normal speech pattern. Their mouths are dry. (Have water handy. Sip, don't gulp.)

People can hear nerves and anxiety.

Preparation and practice reduce your anxiety. Rehearse your key answers over and over. Get comfortable with them. You'll be in a much better position to be given the credibility that you and your COB deserve.

In a live radio interview, make sure you know how long the interview is planned to be and keep an eye on the clock. It will be over before you know it. So don't wait to introduce your key messages. Get them in early and repeat them.

Recording the interview

A seasoned reporter won't have an issue if you wish to record an interview.

If the reporter takes some offence, simply indicate that you'd like to do this to help *you* get better in media interviews.

If your desire to record the interview becomes a deal breaker, it raises serious questions as to whether it's in your COB's best interests to be speaking with this reporter in the first place.

Refusing

Refusing to deal with a media outlet is a serious decision.

It's rare, but if the circumstances warrant, it's OK to ignore their questions, requests for interviews, etc.

If you have lost confidence in their ability to reflect your position fairly and accurately, or if their style and approach provide no opportunity for you to be taken seriously, ignore them.

This may apply to a particular reporter or an entire media outlet.

They will undoubtedly criticize you for it, although in most cases, reasonable people will understand.

Again, this is part of your control of the relationship.

This decision must be carefully considered. I have done this only twice in my long career. Once with a reporter at a major outlet and in the other, an entire publication. In neither case did the decision hurt the COBs for which I worked.

Relationship

It's called media *relations* for a reason. Every media encounter is an opportunity to enhance that relationship.

Treat media people with respect. They have a hard job.

In the vast majority of cases, they will return that respect and be your partner in the relationship.

That said, always remember, their job is to uncover conflict and tell compelling stories. This often runs counter to your objective. That's why it's very much in your best interest to do everything you can to manage your side of the relationship well.

Role of the Media

In its simplest form, the role of the media is to inform. Reporters provide a chronicle of the day's events. They also herald new trends by looking forward and reflect on our history by looking back.

The media also offers opinions of what's right and what's wrong with the world through its columnists and commentators.

S

Saying No, Thank You

There may be times when the circumstances around a media request will be such that your best option is to decline to comment.

It could be a situation in which you are a tangential player in a story, or one in which you cannot effectively advance your COB's position. Politely decline.

Or you may be asked to take on a disproportionate importance in a story, one in which someone else is the key player, but they're not talking and you're next on the list. The media outlet may be looking to have you play a role larger than would otherwise be warranted. You can decline, although if you say yes, you must make it abundantly clear exactly your role and the dominant role of the other party.

The overall lesson here is that saying "No, thank you." is a legitimate position in some circumstances.

Scrums

In a scrum, face the reporter who asked the question and maintain that eye contact. If the question comes from behind or off to one side, acknowledge it, then face a reporter in front of you and answer facing them. What you want to avoid is video of that unflattering angle that has you turned sideways or almost backwards.

As well, in a large news conference or scrum, it may be necessary to repeat the question if not all the media people are in a position to hear it.

Simplicity

Keep your points simple and straightforward. This is not the place to show how smart you are by inserting nuance and complexity into your answers.

Your objective is to be understood.

Social Media

Have a presence in the game. It's not going anywhere anytime soon. Stay on top of its evolution and use it to create or enhance the conversation between your COB and your customers and the world around you. Embrace the opportunities that social media presents for your COB. Yes, it will take time and resources, but done well, it's a huge part of your communications arsenal.

As a "senior practitioner" (I remember when fax machines were seen as space-age miracles...) I've seen a number of my fellow older colleagues shy away from embracing social media and the disruption it brings to media relations. The army of so-called "citizen journalists" and the fact that people in the story are telling the world about it even before you know what's going on, really complicates things.

I got lucky working at the airport, and happened to hire a talented young person who introduced me and the organization to social media, its challenges and benefits.

Speculation

Be very careful when asked to speculate about what your COB might do in the future. Too often, the media, or a faction of their audience, will grab one portion of your answer and declare it to be your intention, sometimes using it to validate their theory of your "hidden agenda".

If there are a few clear cut options ahead of you, declare them.

If the field of options is large and wide, do not speculate.

This is especially true for anything outside your field. Be very careful about offering speculative comments about what someone else might do in a given situation. Stay in your lane.

And...be careful when asked to respond to something somebody else said, unless you are well prepared to do so. If you're not sure, bridge to a key message. "I'm not exactly sure what Ms. Somerset said, or the context of her remarks. The point I want to make is..."

Speed

The faster you talk, the less trustworthy you appear, the less confident in your position you seem to the audience. You are in "selling" mode - you're pitching hard and most audiences will respond negatively.

Sometimes, you're just nervous, and when we're nervous, we tend to speak faster. Thorough preparation will help.

Make a conscious effort to speak slowly. If you think you are speaking too slowly, you're probably right on.

Staking Your Claim

When an issue or crisis presents itself to your COB, get in the game. If you don't stake your claim to your territory and defend that territory with your perspective, your space will be taken over by others – usually your critics.

So don't hesitate. In the olden days, you had several hours to claim your turf. Now you have minutes.

Stereotypes

To expect the media to consistently share your perspectives and ambitions is unrealistic.

They work in a world of stereotypes driven by basic human desires for money, power and sex.

Ask yourself, what stereotypes do you and your COB represent to the media? If unflattering, how can you change it? (The answer to that question usually involves behaving differently. That can be a challenge.)

T

Take Five

Never be pressured by a reporter to make a decision on the spot when your instincts are telling you that what they're asking needs some thought and consideration.

Whether it's to grant an interview or even comment at all on a story, take the time you need to decide.

Even if the request is for background or information about which you are quite confident. You always have the prerogative to take the time to double-check, to confer with colleagues, to step back and think.

Tell the reporter that you need to check and will get back to them in five minutes, or within the hour, whatever. Then be darn sure you keep that promise.

Their pressure is not your pressure. If they push for an answer that second, and you're not completely comfortable with the situation, the answer is no. (If you say no, and they really need you, most often they'll be willing to wait.)

Take Two

If you are doing a taped interview for clips on a newscast, and you make a mistake or stumble badly, or choke - stop talking. Apologize and start over. Go to Take Two.

"Sorry, let me do that again…" Gather yourself and take another run at it.

The reporter wants a good, tight clip and you want to give it to them.

Now, you can't go to Take Ten. You've got to be better prepared than that. The reporter's goal is a good clip. They will be somewhat patient to get it, but they don't have all day.

True confession time. I have done this many times in taped interviews. I found myself wandering, or struggling for the right words and suddenly I've got a tickle in my throat or have to cough. Those few seconds to reset helped me get back on track.

Ts (The Three)

These are easy to remember and are very helpful in constructing your responses to questions. They are:

Simplicity

Clarity

Brevity

Start with these three principles in mind, especially in your initial responses. There are usually plenty of opportunities to expand.

Thank You

In the interests of building a good relationship with the media, it's quite all right to tell a reporter how much you appreciated their fairness and accuracy, when you feel it's appropriate.

We chase them when we think they got it wrong, so letting them know they got it right is only fair on our part. If offered sincerely, it will be appreciated. If offered insincerely, the reporter's finely honed BS detector will go off. If you don't mean it, don't do it.

Remember, it's a relationship.

The Rule

The fundamental rule for all effective communications is:

KNOW YOUR AUDIENCE

Know what they expect from you; know their level of understanding of the issue; know their age; know how many of them there are; know their attitude toward you and your COB.

And, if you can, know their hopes and dreams. What's important to them and their families and communities? Tap into their hearts. Heads will follow.

In other words, know as much as you can about them and use this knowledge to shape not only what you say to them, but your attitude and tone, and the method you use to communicate with them.

The Rule for Communications Advisors

KNOW YOUR SPEAKER

Don't write words that your speaker can't deliver well. Match the tone and language to the speaker.

If they can deliver an inspirational message, write it that way.

If they are a less emotional and operate closer to the ground, lay off the emotion and be more factual.

They may try their best, but in most cases, the message will miss the mark because it's not who they are and their heart won't be in it. Audiences can sense this from a long way off.

You can get a little bit outside their delivery comfort zone, but not much.

Tone

You manage the emphasis you give to certain points by varying the tone, pitch and pace of your voice.

Practice your responses out loud. This rehearsal helps you understand your natural speaking style and adjust accordingly.

As a general rule, when you want to stress a key point,   slow   down.

Traps and Tricks

Some reporters will deliberately try to trick you. Not often, but be prepared.

A reporter says he wants to talk about subject A, but during the interview, passes over that topic quickly and moves to topic B, which is what he's REALLY after, catching you unprepared.

Do not panic. Remember that YOU control the interview. If it is a subject that you are comfortable speaking about, proceed. If not, explain that you have to gather information to answer the question thoroughly and that you will get back to the reporter.

You are asked to provide video "B roll" footage to a reporter who continues to ask questions. (B Roll is extra shots of the interviewee, sometimes walking with the reporter or otherwise engaged, that is used as background visuals during the story.) You may let down your guard, thinking the interview is over.

Remember that EVERYTHING you say and do in the presence of the reporter, from the moment you first meet until they have left the premises is "on the record". Change the subject, or ask the reporter a question.

A request for a simple answer turns into a 10-minute interview.

Be patient and stick to your agenda.

A reporter incorrectly summarizes what you have said, hoping to provoke you into an angry or defensive response.

Patience is the key in these situations. Simply restate your position clearly and succinctly.

Avoid negatives such as "That's not what I said!" Restate your position positively "The most important point is..."

Unless the interview is live, the reporter's inflammatory summary won't make it on air, but your angry answer will.

After you finish answering the question, the reporter simply stares at you, inviting you to continue talking in the hope you'll say something you hadn't meant to and leave yourself vulnerable to attack.

Trusting that you've said everything you want to say in response to the question, simply sit quietly for a moment. If the silence persists, ask the reporter, "Is there anything else you'd like to ask about that?" Put the ball back in their court. They will have to choose to continue with the line of questions or move on.

Trust

Trust people until they give you a reason not to trust them, including the media.

Despite what some believe, the media are *not* always out to get you.

You cannot develop a good working relationship with the media if there is no level of trust. It's a relationship. It's a two-way street.

If your trust is betrayed, you have the option of not dealing with them. You are not obliged to deal with a media outlet if you have no confidence in their ability to reflect your position fairly or accurately. Or, if experience has taught you that you will be skewered regardless of what you say to them.

Don't call them back.

I have taken this position in very few cases. And I have been very comfortable doing it. After all, screw me over once, shame on you. Screw me over twice, then I've given you the benefit of the doubt when I shouldn't have. Screw me over three times, I'm an idiot and I deserve the abuse I will get.

Truth

Tell the truth, as you know it.

Tell as much of it as you can.

Speculation and deceit are not your friends. They will be found out in due course, and your credibility and reputation - what matters most - will be lost.

I once did a presentation at a national public relations conference entitled "Truth – Solid, Liquid or Gas?" My point was that there are many versions of "the truth". And a person can use the truth to mislead an audience by simply omitting some pertinent facts. My "truth" and your "truth" can be very different.

Any "truth" you assert in a media interview must be factual and pass the credibility and reasonableness test the audience will subject it to.

Two Voices

When you are being interviewed, there are two voices you will hear. The external one you are using to answer the questions. And the internal voice – the other voice in your head that's keeping track of what's happening in the interview.

This is the voice that recognizes the opportunity during a question to move to your key message. This is the voice that reminds you to raise a pertinent example. This is the voice that's coaching you as you deliver. It's the voice that tells you whether you're struggling or doing well.

Keep that voice in its place.

If that voice gets too loud, you lose contact with the moment and your focus on listening carefully for your opportunities to deliver your agenda gets drowned out.

If you find yourself listening too much to that voice and you lose contact with the moment and the focus of the question, you can regain your control over that voice a couple of ways, depending on the interview situation.

The easiest is the TV or radio interview being done for clips. Simply ask the reporter to repeat the question, noting that you were distracted for a moment, which is true.

If the interview is live, simply say that "I'm not sure I'm clear on the question, could you repeat it?" The reporter will do so, giving you the precious seconds you need to turn down the volume on the voice in your head and re-focus on your agenda.

U

Unusual

Media people are attracted by the odd and unusual.

When they take a novel angle on something you're doing, don't be too quick to poo-poo the idea.

It could be a great chance to show your COB's human side, poke a little fun at yourself, and show the world you're a real person.

V

Vacuum Theory

When a crisis or significant issue presents itself, a vacuum is created that information needs to fill.

And when you're in the middle of it, you need to fill your part of that information vacuum.

Get in the game. Be available. Stake out your territory, even if you don't have anything terribly comprehensive to contribute. That will come as the situation unfolds.

If you hesitate, others will step in and claim your space in the vacuum as their own, leaving little or none for you. You will be stuck in a reactive role and will be on the defensive right from the start.

Protect yourself and your position by claiming your territory early and holding it throughout the life of the story.

Verbal Cue

This is one of the simplest and most effective techniques in an interview.

When you are gearing up to deliver one of your key messages, tell the world it's coming:

"If I make only one point here today, it is this one…"

"The most important element in this situation is this…"

"Here is the essence of this situation…"

Now, once you've done this, you'd better be prepared to deliver a gem. If you use the verbal cue to foreshadow a weak, irrelevant point, you've wasted it. It's only for the big message at the heart of your story.

And the verbal cue can be very useful if you've managed to talk your way into a corner. Simply say, "I've been rambling around a little bit, let me summarize what I'm trying to say…" And then gather yourself and get back on track.

The verbal cue can be a beautiful thing.

We've all seen this done many times. Listen for it the next time you're watching or listening to a public affairs show.

Video (TV, Podcast, Skype, etc. versus Print)

The fundamental preparations for interviews are the same from one medium to another.

At the same time, there are some differences that must be taken into account. Electronic interviews are usually done within a time restraint and therefore they tend to be shorter and less detailed than print interviews. Print interviews tend to be more open-ended and usually require more background information.

Obviously, video interviews require that thought be given to considerations such as location, dress, grooming and posture. Although these aspects always demand attention, they are more critical in a video situation, where the audience can see you. Research shows that approximately 85% of your communication on video is non-verbal. People judge your credibility by your appearance, *then* they start listening to what you actually are saying.

Posture faux pas:
- slouching
- wild hand or arm gestures
- excessive head or facial movements

Body language negatives:
- folded arms
- leaning back and away from interviewer/camera
- constant fidgeting
- hostile or defensive facial expression

Present yourself as the professional you are.

If you are in a venue other than a studio, ensure the background is neutral/flattering, versus something embarrassing.

Remember Sarah Palin delivering her Thanksgiving interview with a live turkey being slaughtered in the background? Yeah, me too.

Visualization

As part of your interview preparation, make sure you know where it will take place.

If it's on your turf, it's easy to visualize the set up.

If it's in a radio or TV studio with which you're not familiar, arrive in lots of time to get comfortable with the surroundings or even visit the day before, if you can, and get the lay of the land.

Anything you can do to prepare well, is useful.

W

When You Get It Wrong

When you provide the media with information that is inaccurate, despite all your checking and double-checking, you must *immediately* contact every single reporter to whom you gave the inaccurate information, apologize and set the record straight.

How you do this – individual phone calls or general media release/advisory - depends on the situation. But you must do it, and fast.

It's uncomfortable and less than fun, but it must happen. It hurts in the short term, but is an essential element in the development of that trusted working relationship with the media that's so important.

In the "doctor charged with murdering patient" situation in which I was involved, I had been given information by our VP Medical, a doctor himself, about a technical element of the situation that either I misunderstood or he got wrong. When it appeared on the front page of the newspaper the next morning, he came to my office and gave me the bad news.

I had provided this information to four or five reporters the previous day in separate interviews with each.

So, as much as it pained me, I pulled out the media log from the previous day and started the unhappy task of calling each one, correcting the information, saying I was sorry and ensuring they understood the facts properly. Had to be done.

When You're Not Your Best

It's very rare to do a media interview and hit every note just right. In virtually every case, you will look back and think of better ways to say what you said, or a point you missed.

Don't worry about it. Nobody gets it right all the time, every time.

Consider how you could have done better. Learn from the experience. Put it in the memory bank. And be better next time.

Who Speaks When?

As a general rule, use your most articulate subject matter expert, who is well prepared and available.

If it's a low level issue, a corporate communications person ("spokesperson") is fine.

The more impactful the issue, the more necessary it is to have someone with subject matter credibility.

Use your CEO sparingly. They are the last person in line. If they mess up, you've got no one to step in and clean up.

Why Care?

A solid, professional working relationship with the media is in your COB's best interests – especially when things go wrong. And they will.

This solid, professional working relationship also comes in very handy when you want to talk about your latest/greatest product/service.

Effective media relations is crucial to building awareness about your COB. Supportive media stories are valuable third party endorsements and can position your COB as a valuable contributor to the life and growth of your community.

Your goal should be to not only supply useful, newsworthy information to media outlets, but also to build good faith and to develop a solid working relationship with the media.

A good relationship with members of the media is based on trust and honesty. There will be the odd reporter who may violate these principles, but they can be managed.

Good reporters are always looking for help in understanding the situations about which they are reporting. If you can provide that help in an honest, timely and straightforward way, you are in a position to develop a good working relationship with reporters and help them understand what your COB is all about.

Your goal should be to manage your relationship with the media, because you cannot control it. You are one half of a relationship. You can control your side of the relationship, but you can only influence and manage the other side.

X

X-Rated

You may well be tempted to drop in a little salty language in an interview, to spice things up a little.

Don't.

Y

Yes or No

You may find yourself in a situation in which a reporter frames a question and offers you two alternative answers – "yes" or "no".

The fact this question is being asked suggests you're in a confrontational type interview.

And chances are very good that neither answer is particularly useful to you.

For example, "Has your company stopped polluting the river? Yes or no?"

In a perfect world, you are prepared and bridge to the answer you've prepared and are confident in giving. However, it doesn't meet the reporter's "yes or no" criteria.

Should the reporter persist, and ask again, you take the same approach, bridging again to your answer.

Should the reporter refuse to let go, and asks again, "yes or no", you will be sorely tempted to exhibit frustration and anger. Please don't. It will not help. The reporter's badgering will not make it onto the news, but your angry, seemingly petulant answer will.

A favourite response in this situation, delivered with all the politeness and respect you can muster in the moment is, "Bill, I've given you my answer to that question twice. Is there anything else you'd like to ask me about?"

Don't say "I've answered the question twice.", because you haven't. You've given *your* answer to the question.

If the reporter moves on, fine.

If they don't and demand a yes or no response, thank them for their time and politely walk away.

If you are in a scrum situation and the "yes or no" question presents itself, and you've given your answer to the persistent reporter, look to the other reporters and ask, "Is there anything else?"

There are three outcomes to your question:

1. There are no other questions, so you thank them and remove yourself.

2. There are other questions around the topic, outside the "yes or no" question. So you continue the scrum.

3. Others in scrum join in the "yes or no" chorus. In this case, you indicate you've given your answer, thank them and remove yourself.

Z

Zen

Be cool. Channel Rudyard Kipling. "If you can keep your head when all about you are losing theirs and blaming it on you…"

Step outside the issue. Detach.

Emotional responses are rarely helpful. Figure out what's going on, determine what values are in play, and respond thoughtfully and calmly. That's not to say there's no room for emotion. But when emotion is all you've got, your ability to be seen to be taking effective action to fix what's gone wrong will be greatly diminished.

Media Relations 101

- **Your objective is to create and manage a professional working relationship with the media.**

  Demonstrate your respect for reporters and the difficult job they have.

  Trust them, til they give you reason not to.

  Manage this relationship as you would any relationship that's important to you.

- **Media people are friendly, but THEY ARE NOT YOUR FRIENDS**

  Yes, you can have some wonderful chats with media people, but at the end of the day, you are only useful to them as a source. They will use you for their purposes, which is fine, because it's a two-way street and we will use them for our purposes.

- **You control 95% of the interview. And 100% of your answers and attitude.**

- **Be prepared.**

  It's not nearly as difficult as you may think.

- **There is no such thing as "off the record".**

  This information will loop around to bite you. Guaranteed.

  Keep your life simple. Stay on the record.

- **You must have an agenda going into the interview.**

  Questions are easy to anticipate.

  Don't let the question dictate your answer.

- **Objectivity is a myth.**

    Every reporter has their biases. We can only expect them to be fair and accurate.

- **Never say the words "No comment"**

    There are many other ways to convey this message without saying these words.

- **Don't lie or make up answers.**

    Don't say or do anything that you don't want to see, read, or hear in the media.

END